Save Yourself Magazine in the United States of America.

First, 2023.

LETTER FROM THE EDITOR

My Dear Sister,

It is with great pleasure that I introduce to you the inaugural issue of Save Yourself Magazine. This magazine is dedicated to high achieving women who are committed to taking charge of their lives, achieving their goals, and finding fulfillment in all aspects of their lives.

As the editor of this magazine, I am thrilled to bring together a team of writers and experts who share our passion for empowering women. Our content is carefully curated to provide you with practical advice, inspiring stories, and actionable insights to help you overcome obstacles and achieve success on your own terms.

At Save Yourself Magazine, we believe that every woman has the potential to achieve greatness. Our mission is to provide you with the tools and resources you need to unlock that potential and live your best life. Whether you are a career-driven professional, a busy mom, or a young woman just starting out on your journey, we have something for you.

We know that high-achieving women face unique challenges in their personal and professional lives, and our magazine is designed to help you navigate those challenges with confidence and grace. From managing your mental health as a mom, wife & business owner, to nurturing healthy relationships with self and others to providing resources to make it all happen, we are here to help you every step of the way.

I am confident that you will find Save Yourself Magazine to be a valuable resource in your journey to success. Thank you for choosing to join us on this exciting adventure, and I look forward to hearing your feedback and suggestions.

I see you.
I honor you.
I celebrate you.

XOXO,

Dr. Shana

Editor in Chief,
Save Yourself Magazine

Welcome
TO SAVE YOURSELF MAGAZINE!

An unknown writer said "Newsflash! No one is coming to save you! You need to save yourself!"

A lot of us since we were little girls grew up watching cartoons and shows where there was always a "hero"....

There was always someone that came to save the day! No matter how ugly the story of the cartoon and/or show that we were watching, someway- somehow there was a rescue done to save the victim.

Unfortunately, that sometimes is only true in fairytales. Or, is it? Why be left wondering? Why find yourself in the dark?

I have great news! And this is exactly why Dr.Shana has created this momentum magazine to help you learn the strategies and tools that will move you from victim to victor! These strategies can be used in every area of your life to help you become a better you! We want you to be healed from the inside out so that you can be your own superwoman and SAVE YOURSELF!

Dr. Jessica Mosley
Assistant Editor-in-Chief
Save Yourself Magazine

INTERNATIONAL ISSUE 2023

Editorial inquires contact:
info@saveyourselfmagazine.com
Saveyourselfmagazine.com

Contents

EDITOR-IN-CHIEF
Dr. Shana D. Lewis

ASSISTANT EDITOR
Dr. Jessica Mosley

COVER PHOTOGRAPHER
Rashid Tillis
Right Time Solutions Photography

MAKE UP ARTIST
Amethyst Hamilton

CONTRIBUTING WRITERS

LaShasta Bell
Paula Gray
Jenequa Eldridge
Amethyst Hamilton
Tina Hamm
Charlene Jackson
LaQuondra Levias

Shadawn McCants
LaTonda Page
Dr. Stacy Peebles
Jamie Sanderson Reid
Dr. Kimberly Sims
Cherisse Singh
Nisa Williams

Healing Doesn't Happen Overnight

Embracing the Journey to Wholeness

By Shadawn McCants

The process of healing, whether physical, emotional, or psychological, is a gradual and often complex journey. In today's world we are living in the era of go-go-go. Heck I am even guilty. One of my favorite mantras is "ALL GAS NO BREAKS." And as I write this piece I am reminded of the mindset and energy that it takes to live up to that. Despite society's longing for a quick fix, true healing requires time, patience, and self-awareness. Understanding that healing doesn't happen overnight is vital to accepting and embracing the journey to wholeness. In this article, we will explore the various aspects of the healing process with respect to mind, body and spirit and provide guidance for those seeking a path toward living wholly from the inside out.

The Importance of Time in the Healing Process

One of the most significant factors in any healing process is time. The human body and mind are incredibly resilient, but they require time to repair

and rebuild after experiencing trauma, injury, or emotional distress. Imagine the time it takes for a 3rd degree burn to heal...weeks, months and for some years. Same goes for the journey of healing. It is essential to honor the natural process and give ourselves the time we need to heal. Pressuring ourselves to recover faster than our body or mind is ready can lead to additional stress and hinder the healing process.

Patience and Self-Compassion

As we navigate the healing journey, it's crucial to practice patience and self-compassion. Healing is not a linear process, and we may experience setbacks and challenges along the way. By treating ourselves with kindness and understanding, we can learn to foster a safe and nurturing environment for growth and recovery.

It's helpful to remind ourselves that setbacks are a normal part of the healing process and that it's okay to not be okay. Acknowledging and accepting our current state can help us shift our perspective and make room for the healing to flow.

The Role of Support Networks

One of the most valuable resources on our journey to wholeness is the support of those around us. Friends, family, and professionals can provide encouragement, understanding, and guidance during our most challenging moments. It's important to seek out these support networks and allow ourselves to be vulnerable, as opening to others can create a sense of connection and help alleviate feelings of isolation. Collective healing is powerful.

Developing a self-care routine can also be an essential part of the healing process. Engaging in activities that promote relaxation, mindfulness, and overall well-being can help provide a strong foundation and maintenance for healing.

The Power of Incremental Progress

While it's easy to become overwhelmed by the magnitude of our healing journey, focusing on incremental progress can be a powerful and effective strategy. Breaking down our goals into smaller, manageable steps can help us maintain motivation and a sense of accomplishment.

Every day, we can take small actions that contribute to our overall well-being. These actions may include journaling, practicing mindfulness, engaging in physical activity, or seeking professional support. As we consistently prioritize our healing, we will begin to see the cumulative effect of these small steps, ultimately leading to wholeness.

The Role of Forgiveness

Forgiveness is a critical aspect of the healing process, both in terms of forgiving ourselves and others. Holding onto past hurts and resentments can hinder our progress and perpetuate a cycle of pain. By letting go of these negative emotions, we create space for healing and growth.

Forgiveness doesn't mean condoning harmful behavior or forgetting the impact of past events. Instead, it's about recognizing the power of releasing the burden of anger, bitterness, and resentment, allowing ourselves to move forward in our journey. Remember forgiveness is for you not them.

Finding Strength in the Healing Process

Embracing the reality that healing doesn't happen overnight can be challenging, but it's also an opportunity for growth and self-discovery. Through the ebbs and flows of the healing process, we develop resilience, courage, and inner strength that can serve us in all aspects of life.

As we learn to navigate the complexities of our healing journey, we become more equipped to face future challenges from a space of awareness, self-compassion and love creating a strong foundation for you to flourish and live authentically, unapologetic, and whole.

In conclusion, healing is a multi-faceted and often arduous process but one I promise is worth every moment.

Shadawn McCants, is a Licensed Professional Counselor turned Healologist. She specializes in helping individuals heal from the inside out. You can connect with her via all social media platforms under her full name or email at healinginyourheels@gmail.com.

#Every Heel has a Sole and Every Soul Needs Healing

AIN'T NOBODY COMING TO SAVE YOU

By Dr. Shana D. Lewis

Ladies, forgive my bad English but let's begin with a few truths.

1. Ain't nobody coming to save you.

2. Even if they tried to save you, you'd think they didn't do it right and you'd do it over anyway.

3. It's always been your job, and always will be your job. So get back to work!

Here are the facts. Women all over the world have spent their entire life serving others. We have forgotten about ourselves and made everyone else a priority in our lives. We have single handedly decided that if we don't do it, no one else will so we do everything, all the time. And when we find ourselves depleted of all energy and with little to no reserve, operating from what I call -E (less than nothing), we will blame 'them' for all of it. While that will allow us to feel justified in our resentfulness or even anger toward others in our lives, it doesn't come close to addressing the real problem. The real problem is that we have not taken full responsibility for our current state of being. If we are not well, mentally, physically, or emotionally, we truly do not get to blame anyone else for it.

If we are responsible for our wellness, or lack thereof, then we also have the capacity to do something about it. If we are waiting on someone else to change, or be kind, or to offer assistance we have given our power away. I want us all to get clear on the reality that no one else can save you like you can. Let's take a look at what this really means.

What does it truly mean to save yourself you might ask? Here are a few of the important key points to consider.

Saving yourself means…

You value yourself enough as someone/ something worthy of being saved.

Too often as women we lack the self-love and confidence needed to actually put ourselves first. If asked this question directly, I have not met a woman who would say openly that she doesn't value herself. However, if you look at how you treat yourself in regard to self-care, then it becomes clearer. Those who value and love themselves more will take better care of themselves. Those of us who don't…won't. I realize there are many excuses we may give as to why we can't or don't but this is the reality. The thing you value more…you will take care of. Period.

Saving yourself means…

You understand that your wellness is the foundation of your capacity to show up in power for everyone else in your world.

I make the statement often, If mama ain't right, ain't nobody right. I say this, not as a cliché but because if we are not well, then we do not have what we need to adequately serve those we are called to serve whether this be family, work, ministry, etc. We will try but the outcomes will not be as great or as powerful as they would be if we were operating from a full cup. The empty cup service must stop. We must intentionally fill ourselves sufficiently so that we can serve from a place of overflow or what I like to call saucerlife.

Saving yourself means…

Putting yourself first, no guilt and no apology

The position you find yourself in, in your life is completely up to you. No one can make you last unless you allow it to occur. Putting ourselves first, is truly a critical component of saving ourselves because if we are last on the list of 'to-dos' then we will find ourselves out of time, energy and resources to actually do the saving we need done. And then what happens is..we are left depleted and the outcome is poor.

Saving yourself means...

Deciding for yourself that you are the one you have been waiting for.

You decide that you are not looking for anyone else to come save you. In fact you don't want anyone else to save you because they don't have the capacity to save something they did not create. We know that God is a Savior, and he is the only savior. He has given us the power to make decisions for ourselves that allow us to function in the path he has created for our lives.

As you think about this concept, Save Yourself, remember that saying in the airplane, 'Put your mask on first.' The reason for this is simple. If you don't have a mask on and cabin pressure drops low enough you could become unconscious, pass out and be rendered helpless to anyone else in need. And your attempts to put them first will actually have the opposite effect you were hoping for. Choose today to Save You.

Order Your Copy!
www.SelfcareisthenewSEXY.com

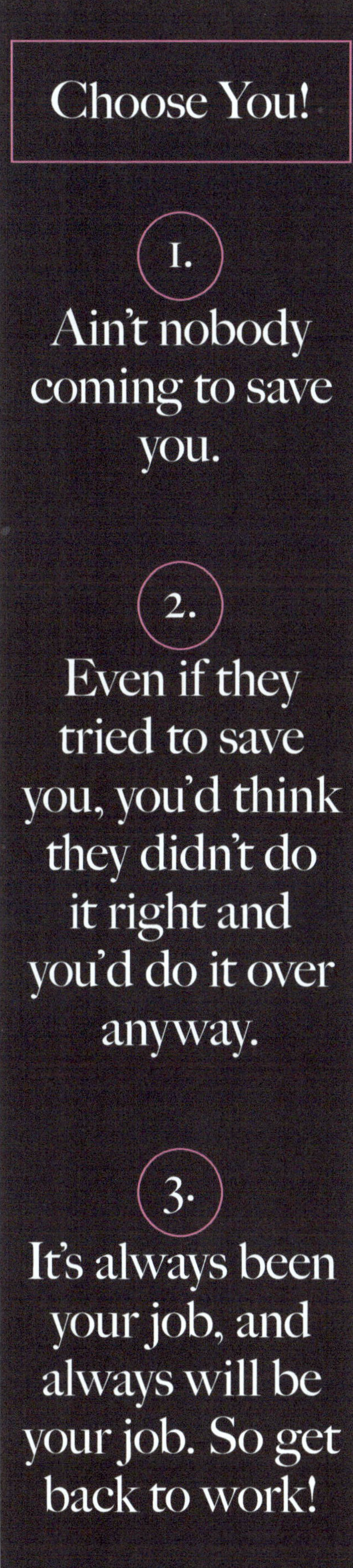

It is time for black women to redefine what it means to be "strong".

Creating Healthy Boundaries

By Dr. Stacy Peebles

For generations black women have held the community together. We have accomplished this through hard work, dedication and sacrifice. Most of us have heard the term, "Strong Black Woman" and many of us have used this term to proudly describe ourselves or to proclaim our independence.

We have endured discrimination and racial trauma while also dealing with issues of sexism and double standards that come with being a woman. We are pulled in many directions as the "go-to" person for multiple people in our lives. It may sometimes feel like you can't catch a break and the thought of saying no or disappointing someone feels impossible.

For so long being strong as a black woman has meant suffering in silence. We must now use our strength for self-preservation. We must save ourselves. This self-preservation will actually enable us to be more effective in our many roles and decrease our level of stress. This may seem like a daunting task but here are a few tips to help you get started.

· Recognize your worth. Fight the urge to believe that your needs don't matter.

· Employ positive self-talk. Speak positivity into your life. Recognize that your words and thoughts have power. Be kind to yourself.

· Decide what your deal breakers are then refuse to accept any of these things in your life.

· Learn to say no without feeling a need to provide an explanation

· Accept that other people do not need to agree with or understand the boundaries that you put in place.

As "strong black women" we must learn to put our needs first. You cannot pour from an empty cup. One of the first steps in self-preservation is putting consistent boundaries in place that help protect your health and peace of mind. Creating effective boundaries is an amazing act of self-love and strength.

Dr. Stacy Nakia Peebles (Dr. Stacy), is an Emotional Wellness Practitioner with extensive experience providing services to individuals seeking support in navigating through life's challenges. Dr. Stacy's goal is to empower clients to make positive and informed decisions that will lead to a sense of well-being and serenity. Dr. Stacy takes a holistic approach to health care, with a focus on promoting a sense of self-love and empowering clients to live the meaningful life that they deserve. Dr. Stacy, is a Licensed Psychotherapist (LCSW), Certified Empowerment Coach, Certified Kemetic Reiki Practitioner and Reiki Master. Visit beingdrstacy.com.

By Nisa K. Williams

EMOTIONAL INTELLIGENCE

The only thing more empowering than being an entrepreneur, is being a woman entrepreneur. Currently, 42% of US businesses are owned by women, and with women being the most educated gender in the US, we are poised to raise that percentage exponentially over the next few years.

Competition is fierce and education and technical know-how can no longer be the leading drivers of success. High social and emotional intelligence (EQ) is now one of the most important skills needed by entrepreneurs; even more so than IQ or hard-skills. Fortunately, EQ is something that can be learned and improved upon.

EQ refers to the ability to recognize, understand and manage one's own emotions, as well as the emotions of others. It includes essential entrepreneurial skills such as self-awareness, self-regulation, and motivation. Women often feel overwhelmed with the many roles that we fill such as mother, caregiver, spouse, employee, friend, ect.. Because of this, women entrepreneurs may be more susceptible to disruptive emotions and mindsets that can hinder consistent progress or cause us to stall altogether. Doubt, fear and imposter syndrome are just a few of the disruptive emotions that have a tendency to block entrepreneurial success. Increasing one's EQ will help you to recognize and transform the disruptive emotions, mindsets, and limiting beliefs so that you can excel beyond your own expectations.

Consider some of the following activities to begin increasing your EQ: 1) Observe and be honest about your emotions as they occur. 2) Pay attention to how you respond to stressors and be intentional about making productive decisions. 3) Discover the triggers that cause you to shut down or procrastinate. 4) Practice true self-care. 5) Talk to an experienced coach who can help guide the self-discovery and growth process to propel you forward. If you are an entrepreneur who struggles with motivation, consistency, self-doubt or fear, improving your EQ is a critical step on your road to success.

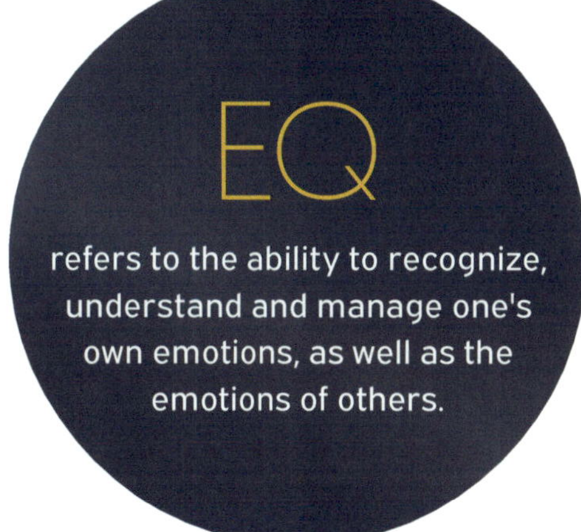

As a certified Social and Emotional Intelligence Coach, I facilitate workshops for entrepreneurs that cover all aspects of Social and Emotional Intelligence. Visit my website www.nisawilliamsassociates.com for more information.

Permission to Priortize
YOU!

Overcoming stress and burnout
with **Jenequa Eldridge**

Jenequa Eldridge, CPC, is a Gallup®-Certified Strengths Coach, Corporate Trainer, Corporate Speaker, and Executive Coach, with over 20 years of award-winning experience as a corporate system change agent.

Who is Jenequa Eldridge and what makes your story special?

I am a woman of God who is dedicated to showing people how to aim their gifts at their goals. So many people believe that if they could only fix their weaknesses, they could achieve success. This is the furthest thing from the truth, weakness fixing may prevent some failures but a focus on what you do well is what leads to success. I had to learn this the hard way. I was in a position where I was operating from a depleted space. I was burnt out, frustrated, sick, and tired. When I say sick, I don't mean that figuratively...I suffered a stroke due to the stress that accompanied my quest to show up like my predecessor had and to do things the way she had done them. It wasn't until I discovered my talents and invested in them to become true strengths, that I achieved true success in my role and became the award-winning change agent for my organization whose impact has outlived my tenure with the company.

What is your favorite affirmation?

Today I will enter every space knowing that I am competent and capable to make valuable contributions that will leave them better than I found them.

What does 'Save Yourself' mean to you, and how have you done this in your lifetime?

I believe that saving yourself means that you proactively guard your wellbeing. I refuse to be complicit in my own demise, so I am intentional with my presence and my energy. If we are not valued in a space, then we will not show up.

How does the work that you do help women to 'Save Themselves'?

I help women get to know themselves so that they can disrupt burnout and operate from a place of strength.

What have been your greatest barriers or struggles in life, business, and personal growth and how did you overcome them?

My greatest struggle has been my tendency to silo my struggles and challenges by only sharing the good stuff. I have been intentional to overcome this by creating accountability partnerships with women who share my passion for impact and legacy. We have curated a safe space where we can be vulnerable and open about our challenges.

What advice would you give to your younger self about wellness, selfcare, and prioritizing yourself if you could go back in time?

No is a whole sentence, and you don't need anyone's permission to prioritize your own wellbeing.

What would you say to a woman who is struggling to find balance in her life between herself, family, and career?

I would tell her that balance is an unrealistic goal. Harmony is a more realistic aim. Also, harmony is what feels good to you and your family. Unimpacted individuals don't get a vote.

What are your favorite ways to pour back into yourself mind, body, spirit?

I pour into my: mind with silence or a good book, body with a good swim, and spirit with good music.

What can readers expect from you in the upcoming months?

In the upcoming months my accountability partners and I are launching an app that will connect individuals who are looking to build impactful accountability partnerships.

How can readers connect to you and support your work on social media and other platforms?

IG - @JenequaEldridgeCPC
LinkedIn - @JenequaEldridgeCPC
Facebook - @JenequaEldridgeCPC
www.JenequaEldridge.com

UNBOX THE DETOX:
STOP THE MUSTERBATION, AND START SLIVING, BABE!

By Cherisse Singh

While it's important to have focused life goals and work towards achieving them, it becomes problematic when we approach vision boards and to-do lists as "must-haves" or "have-to" obligations, leading to what is referred to as "MUSTerbation."

Filling our lives with endless "MUSTerbations" can result in anxiety, depression, and various other mental health issues. Dr. Albert Ellis, Ph.D., the father of Rational Emotive Behavior Therapy (REBT), defines the emotional and mental strain caused by these "must-haves" as MUSTerbation.

Before getting trapped in the cycle of "MUSTerbations," it's time to detox and rediscover the enjoyment of slaying both our personal and professional lives. Let's start "Sliving," a combination of slaying and living, babe.

A successful detox involves cleansing the body, recalibrating the mind, balancing emotions, and synergizing energies.

LET'S BEGIN THE DETOX:

1. CLEANSING THE BODY:

Adopting an anti-inflammatory and low-carb lifestyle is the fastest way to rest and detoxify the body. This approach helps break carb addiction and reset our gut mycobiome.

2. RECALIBRATING THE MIND:

Being fully present in the moment and letting go of fear and regret creates emotional balance. Meditation, contemplation techniques, and gratitude journaling can help recalibrate the mind and enhance mental fitness.

3. BALANCING EMOTIONS:

Consciously recognizing our triggers and developing strategies to reduce or change our responses can help achieve emotional balance. "Nighttime Review" journaling is a helpful practice that allows us to identify triggers, evaluate our responses to these emotions, and develop effective ways to respond if triggered again.

4. SYNERGIZING ENERGIES:

Maintaining a positive energy flow throughout our body and life improves overall health and wellness. Managing our Chi, Prana, or Aura creates an environment for our body and mind to thrive. Simple exercises and breathing techniques found in practices like Yoga, Tai Chi, and Pranayama fuel positive energy.

By embracing this detox, we can free ourselves from the pressures of "MUSTerbations" and cultivate a more balanced and fulfilling life. Let's unbox the detox, slay our goals, and truly enjoy living, babe.

CS FAB
Cherisse Singh is a Fashion & Beauty Journalist, Global Fashion Marketing strategist, and Body Contouring Specialist. She is also a Holistic Health and Wellness Coach, specializing in Keto, Yogic, and Intermittent Fasting methods.Scan QR Code for more wellness tips!

Sisterhood and Self Care

By Paula R. Gray

Don't take your girlfriends for granted. Below are five ways to be more intentional in your friendships.

Engage Her Dreams

Get excited about what your friends are doing. Whether it's in their personal or professional life, be present for the big and small moments. Engagement looks like supporting their businesses, checking up on them, holding them accountable, praying for them, sending food, watching the kids, or pitching in whatever way benefits them.

Employ Listening

There will be times when your friends will need your opinion, and they will ask you for it. But there will be other times when a listening ear is all that your friends desire. At that moment, they don't want you to analyze anything. As a loving friend, you honor that. Sharing their heart with you allows your friends an opportunity to process their thoughts in a safe and loving space.

Exalt the Relationship

Keep the connection tight. Friends require time with you no matter how long you've known each other. They know you care but it's so nice to meet up, catch up on a video chat or even take a girl's trip. Carving out time for friends in your productive schedules benefits you and them. A good time refreshes everyone's soul.

Encourage Her

Each of your friends has special qualities that you adore. From time to time, remind them of why they're important to you. They may be great listeners, push you out of your comfort zone, check you when your spirit is wrong, or make you laugh when you're feeling down. Let your friends know they are significant and add value to your life.

Exercise Honesty

Your friends will appreciate the truth, especially since they love and respect you. If you have an issue with a friend, be honest. If she asks for your opinion, tell the truth. If you see her struggling emotionally, address it. Sometimes delivering hard truths makes things uncomfortable for a moment. But true friendships can withstand any storm if the foundation is built on honesty.

Paula R. Gray is a woman of faith who loves to see other women winning. She is a wife, mother and author of several books published on Amazon.com. Contact Paula on Facebook at Paula R. Flatts-Gray or on Instagram at prgray_89.

Hey, Sis,

It's no secret that we live in a day and age where beauty is often simplified to the impossible standards set by social media. We are constantly bombarded by images of manufactured bodies, faces caked with makeup, and inches of weave that would shatter the average woman's bank account with one transaction. Though this faction of reality rings of doom and gloom for the natural beauty, there is actually a remnant of those who choose to walk in their God given image to truly embrace who they are.

As a professional makeup artist, it is always my goal to enhance the natural beauty that God gave you, never to transform it. With this in mind, I want to propose this critical thought:

"The beauty of self care exists within our perfect imperfections."

Sis, I want to challenge you to love yourself just the way you are and this following exercise will give you the space to do just that.

Take the next five minutes to yourself, light a candle, take a seat and look at the beautiful creation in the mirror.

Embrace all of the perfect imperfections whether it be a dark circle, a wrinkle, a scar, an enlarged pore, a zit or two. Let's go a little deeper and think about how those perfect imperfections came about. I'd like for you to take a moment before going down a rabbit hole to recognize how long you've been living with them and now you've since mustered up the resilience to continue to accomplish life's many tasks.

Let's shift and take a look at some of your favorite features: those beautiful full lips, those lengthy lashes, bomb brows, high cheekbones. God did his thing with those, didn't he? He also did his thing with the not so loved areas. In this effort he created this perfectly imperfect being for such a time as this.

Now that we've completed this exercise, I pray you see that there is beauty in balancing the perfectly imperfect. The imperfectly seen pieces are just the beginning of a beautiful story and that story, or your face in this case, can easily be enhanced by just a touch of self care whether that be through a daily skin care ritual, an occasional makeup application or even a daily makeup routine.

Sis, I want you to realize that it's okay to use various tools and techniques to perfect the imperfect areas, however what's most important is ensuring that you approach those areas with genuine care and most importantly authentic love for you.

We'll continue this journey next time covering the how, but until then, continue to love on you.

Fearfully and wonderfully made,

– Amethyst.

Amethyst N. Hamilton is a Houston based makeup artist, beauty educator, cosmetic personal shopper with a passion of enhancing natural God given beauty. With over 10 years industry experience, she has truly embraced her calling for makeup artistry but also coaching trailblazing women to step boldly and beautifully in the skin they're in. IG @ amethystnaomi.

SELF CARE IS THE NEW *Sexy*

By Dr. Shana Lewis

You have run yourself ragged enough for long enough. That hamster wheel is about to swing off the hinges and the truth is the people you are running yourself ragged for may not appreciate the level of sacrifice you've decided to give them. You've sacrificed your mind, your body and your spirit. And now it's time to get your SEXY back!

What is SEXY you might ask. Let's first dispel the idea that SEXY is all about what we look like. As it relates to self-care it has nothing to do with that at all. When we have cared for ourselves adequately and sufficiently, we are truly able to show up in power for ourselves and those we are called to serve. When we have had adequate sleep, have organized our world, drink plenty of water, exercise, and set those good old boundaries with folks, we can enter any room with confidence.

This is what SEXY is all about.

When I am well, I am clear, focused and know who I am and what I require. This allows me to ask for what I need without any guilt. I show up for everyone else day in and day out and today is my day to show up for me. No guilt. No apology. Sis today is your day too.

The problem many of us, high achieving women have is that we have bought into the idea that we are supposed to be the answer to everyone's issue, and it is wrong for us to put ourselves first. Well, I don't buy that at all. Serving from a deficit place, or empty cup doesn't serve anyone well. We can only truly serve well from that place of abundance or what I like to call #saucerlife.

It's time for you sis to walk into your abundant place and choose you for once. Getting your SEXY back allows you to be the best version of you therefore increasing your ability to serve in power for those in your world. There are so many things you can do to start this process, but I will share my favorite with you here. Start your morning off right.

How many of you have a morning routine? This one thing is what has literally changed the trajectory of my entire life. Pre-pandemic I didn't have a morning routine. Well, if you call getting up 5 minutes late and jumping and running around like a chicken minus my head, then OK I had one. But seriously, when I realized the value of creating time for breathing every morning and mediation it changed the game for me. I am now able to begin my day with intention, focus and purpose by meditating

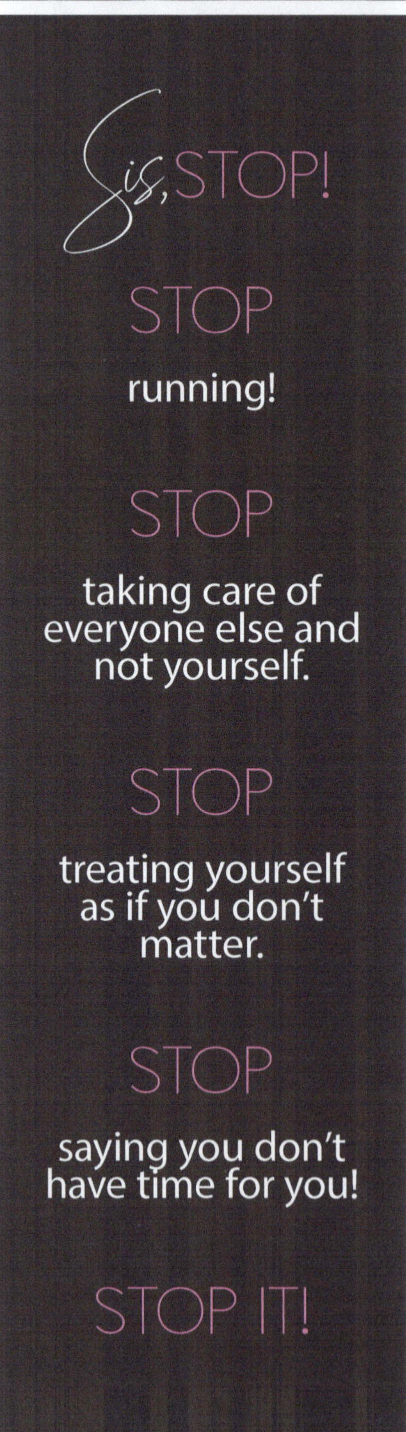

and breathing at the top of the morning. In addition to this devotion must be a part of my morning. I can do absolutely nothing without being connected to my power source FIRST.

Some women have said that they don't think they have time for a morning routine like this. I challenge you to consider carving out 5-10 minutes just to start. You don't need an extra hour sis. 5-10 minutes a day will make a significant difference in how you feel. I promise. Take a few minutes right now to write down one thing you can do in the morning that will support you more. It might just be breathing, meditation, or journaling. That is fine. Don't add too much too fast because you won't do it anyway. 1% increments of change are all we need.

Dr. Shana D. Lewis is an Executive Wellness Coach and the Editor in Chief of Save Yourself Magazine. Stay connected saveyourselfmagazine.com

Write one new morning routine activity here:

____

____

____

How many days per week would you like to do this activity? (Remember it may not be every day if that's not possible so decide what makes sense)

____

____

What resources do you need to make this activity happen?

____

____

____

____

TIP: Think about getting up 5 minutes earlier, going to bed 30 minutes earlier, preparing lunch the night before so you have more time or getting clothes laid out early etc.

Next make a post and share it with the _Save Yourself Magazine_ FB page or tag us on IG @saveyourselfmag so we can celebrate you for taking the first action step toward saving yourself.

Get all the SEXY plays needed to get your SEXY back make sure you grab a copy of my Selfcare is the New SEXY the Playbook and Workbook at: selfcareisthenewsexy.com

The Journey to Sacred Self Care Through the Seasons:
The Spring Edition

By LaTonda Page

Sacred Self-Care is a commitment to align with the authentic version of yourself through mindset transformation. This adventurous transformational process produces a lifestyle of purpose, love and power. The Sacred Self-Care lifestyle focuses on "BEing" as opposed to "DOing" tasks and activities only.

The Sacred Self-Care journey necessitates establishing a foundation that nourishes your mind, body and spirit holistically. The foundation consists of intentional breathing, prayer, meditation, journaling, body movements and scheduled solitude. As these six practices become rituals of your daily life, it produces a firm foundation and permits self-rediscovery.

As you contemplate methods of self-rediscovery, being in alignment with the elements of the season can contribute to creating holistic approaches to Sacred Self-Care. The Spring season evokes awakenings, seed planting and new beginnings. By incorporating these elements, it can assist in the Journey to Sacred Self-Care through the Spring Season.

The first segment of the Journey to Sacred Self-Care requires contemplation of the six foundational practices. If Sacred Self-Care is a new concept, consider using this season of new beginnings to develop your practices. If the six foundational practices are already embodied into your lifestyle, take time to reflect whether adjustments are necessary for this season.

Next, use these introspective prompts to begin expanding your holistic approach:

> *Mind* – Are your thoughts inspiring or disorderly?
> What old thoughts/beliefs do you need to release and replace with new ones?
>
> *Body* – What is your body telling you that she needs during this season? How will you honor the request of your body?
>
> *Spirit* – Who are you at your core?
> Is your inner and outer life congruent? Why or why not?

The last segment of this journey requires a merging of the six foundational practices with the holistic approach into your daily life. For example, you may create gratitude statements for the mind, incorporate stretching for the body and recite "I am" affirmations for the spirit. The steps of the Journey to Sacred Self-Care need to be utilized consistently, however the holistic approach will be individualized for your unique life redesign.

Additional information may be obtained at: thehealingspaceforblackwomen.com

Greetings! My name is **LaTonda Page**, the Founder & CEO of The Healing Space for Black Women. I am a Sacred Self-Care Facilitator and a Mental Health and Wellness Advocate. The Healing Space for Black Women is a virtual village created to cultivate holistic wellness for Black Women worldwide. Currently, I offer educational workshops, individual and community sessions virtually.

WELLNESS is SEXY

By Kim Sims, MD

If I had a dollar for every person that asked me why they were tired, I could probably retire. My evaluation for fatigue spans a variety of causes, yet many times, boils down to a common denominator.

I dig into a history on that poised, professional woman, and I generally hear a similar story— she's excelling at work and home but doesn't have time for something as basic as eating lunch.

I leave this woman with tools I'll share with you— the foundation to keeping it SEXY.

S-Sleep

Adults need 7-9 hours of sleep nightly to maintain health. When we don't get this, there is the obvious: fatigue, brain fog, and moodiness. However, it also puts you at risk for insulin resistance (which causes diabetes), elevated blood pressures, heart disease, obesity, infection, and mood disorders—and that's not an exhaustive list.

Just one night of inadequate sleep can harm your thinking and cortisol levels, and it can take up to one week to make up for it.

E-Eat Well

Eat more plants and whole foods, and less sugar. More studies are showing the harms of highly processed and high sugar foods. Remember, you get out what you put in.

X-eXercise and Activity

The goal active lifestyle is defined as 150 minutes of moderate-intensity or 75 minutes of high-intensity cardiovascular exercise weekly plus strength and stretch training. The important things to know: do something you love and every little bit counts. In as little as 7 minutes a day, you can reap benefits such as improved energy, thinking, mood, and decreased risk of dying from cardiovascular disease.

Y-You Time

Make time to meditate, focus on things you love, and feed your spirituality. Wellness is mind, body, and spirit, so we can't neglect any of these and think that we're going to feel our best.

When we hit that brick wall of overwhelm and fatigue, it's generally because we've decided to prioritize something or someone over the foundational elements required for our well-being. No more. Affirm today: I am a treasure that deserves proper maintenance and care.

Kim Sims, MD is a physician specializing in Internal Medicine and weight management, author, speaker, wife, mom and wellness champion. She is passionate about empowering women to break up with the superwoman syndrome to embrace not just their wellness, but in it, their power, purpose, and peace.

SLEEP
IS MY
SUPERPOWER

By Lashasta Bell, LPC

I am sure you have heard of the term "superpower"? I know it can be associated with superheroes and fiction, but I also believe that sleep gives me superpowers. As a high achieving woman, running multiple businesses I find myself juggling a lot of responsibilities and tasks throughout my day. I know how hard it is to make time for yourself. After all, there's nothing more important than putting in the hours and getting things done! But I've learned something that not many people talk about: sleep can be your secret weapon when it comes to productivity and performance. That's why I'm here to tell you why sleep is my superpower. To make sure I can keep up with all the demands, sleep has been the one thing that helps me soar.

I get it—you want to make the most of every moment in your day. But if you really want to see results from your efforts, then making time for sleep is everything. Set yourself a bedtime goal—even if it's just 15-30 minutes earlier than usual—and stick with it every night, yes even during the weekend! Once you get into the habit of going to bed on time each night, trust me—you'll start noticing a difference in your energy levels and focus during the day. It may seem counterintuitive at first, but giving yourself permission to go to bed will actually free up more time later on when you're not struggling against fatigue or trying to rework sloppy mistakes due to lack of focus. As a high achieving woman who needs to stay productive in order to succeed, I prioritize getting enough sleep (my sweet spot is 7.5-8 hours) so that I am energized and ready for whatever comes my way during the day.

I have also noticed that getting quality sleep helps me retain information better than when I don't get enough restful sleep. When we are well rested our brains are better able to store and recall information from memory more easily because it's less distracted by fatigue or fatigue-related symptoms like headaches or joint pain. I find myself recalling details from conversations more easily or facts faster when needed for personal and professional purposes.

Once you reclaim your time and start to get quality sleep each night, prepare yourself for some major benefits! Not only will you notice an improvement in mental clarity and physical energy levels during the day, but studies have found that getting enough sleep also helps reduce stress and anxiety levels significantly over time. And don't forget about those creative juices – chances are they'll flow a lot smoother once you give yourself permission to snooze each night!

Sleep really does give us superpowers! Not only does it help us stay energized throughout the day, increase our creativity and productivity but it also enhances memory retention which is essential for success as a high achieving woman. Prioritizing good quality sleep each night should be at the top of every woman's list if she wants to achieve her goals and have the energy to celebrate. So close your eyes tonight knowing that tomorrow you will wake up with new super powers waiting for you!

LaShasta Bell is a woman living intentional to secure her peace, rest and sleep. She's a mom to two sons and has been married for 20+ years. LaShasta is a certified sleep coach better known as The Professional Sleep Strategist. She is also licensed professional counselor and certified anxiety treatment professional.

20 Affirmations for MOMS

By LaQuondra Levias

1. I am doing the best that I can with what I have.
2. There is no right or wrong way to do it. I'm doing it my way!
3. I don't have to be perfect; I just have to be present.
4. Progress is the goal, not perfection.
5. Perfect doesn't exist.
6. I have a plan, but I can go with the flow.
7. I love my child/ren even when I don't like them.
8. It's ok if they cry!
9. I deserve a break.
10. Self-care is not selfish.
11. I choose joy.
12. My child/ren deserves a rested and happy mother.
13. It takes a village; let them participate.
14. It's ok to ask for help.
15. It's ok to say no....to your partner, your friends, your job, your parents, your in-laws, to anything that doesn't feel right.
16. My body may look different, but I have a human life to show for it.
17. I will not compare myself to other moms. Every mom is different.
18. I am more than a mom.
19. I'm still me!
20. This too shall pass.

LaQuondra, a proud boy mom of 2, is a licensed professional counselor in Texas. She owns and operates U Can Too Professional Counseling Service, focusing on helping adult individuals and couples unpack past grievances and plan for the future they desire.

ucantoocounseling.com
LLevias@uncantoocounseling.com

M indfulness continues to be a compelling approach for reducing stress, anxiety, anger, and trauma. When utilized effectively and consistently anyone can benefit from practicing mindfulness from children to adults. There are many misconceptions about mindfulness and many people think mindfulness is a very simple approach that can't begin to address their very big problems. Clients have remarked, "I can't breathe my way out of this one." As it relates to the misconception that breathwork is too simple of a technique to aide with problems that seem to be overwhelming and debilitating. It is important to remember that mindfulness is not a quick fix, as with any new skill, it takes commitment and continued effort to experience the benefits and its true effectiveness. One of the benefits of mindfulness is an increased awareness of stress triggers and learning how to manage and respond to them. Emotional regulation, a by-product of mindfulness, can contribute to significantly improving relationships not only with self, but with others. Regular mindfulness practices can help train your brain to stay focused and avoid distractions.

Beginner tips for getting started with mindfulness:

1. Don't be defeated by internal chatter when you meditate instead notice the thoughts as they arise and write them down.

2. Start small but be consistent by practicing a few minutes each day and gradually increase your duration over time.

3. Be patient with yourself and practice self-compassion if you find yourself struggling to stay focused or becoming self-critical.

One of the most important steps in self-compassion is mindfulness-a state of being aware of your challenges and discomfort without judgment. A mindfulness practice you can implement today is writing with your non-dominant hand. Create an affirmation and write it 10 times with your non-dominant hand. The goal is to engage in the process without judgment while noting the level of focus needed to make the writing legible. Breathwork, another mindfulness practice, aids in relaxing the body, improving mood, sleep, and decreasing anxiety. Deep breathing or belly breathing is a great starting point for engaging in this practice.

Charlene M. Jackson, LPC, LCDC, is a mental health therapist located in Austin, Texas specializing in anxiety, depression, relational issues, and developmental trauma. If you or someone you know are interested in getting start with therapy or mental health coaching, please visit mosaiccwcom.com for more information about getting started with services.

The Journey from Loss to Purpose

By Tina Hamm

Peacefully perched on my porch, nestled at an elevation of 225 feet in the majestic mountains of St. Maarten, I find myself reflecting on a profound lesson that has transformed the trajectory of my life. It is the principle of living consciously and intentionally, driven solely by purpose and embodying the highest expression of why we are born.

People often inquire how a single woman born in North Carolina and raised in Washington, D.C., managed to uproot her life and relocate 2000 miles away at the age of 58. The catalyst for this significant change was the devastating stroke my partner suffered in his brain stem, leading to his passing on December 26, 2017. As someone who identifies as a spiritual being having a human experience, I believed I had confronted my grief. However, it was during a chance conversation with my friend and therapist in January 2019 that I experienced a profound revelation: "Throughout my life, I had been a gardener, but it was time to become a flower." Trusting the wisdom and depth of Dr. Jerel Eaglin's counsel, I listened without overthinking.

Following his sage advice, I made the decision to close my catering and event planning business, which had thrived for 25 years, and accepted a coveted management position with Occasions Caterers—an entirely new experience for me. It was humbling to step into a "job" after such a long time, but it also brought relief from stress and proved to be a deeply rewarding endeavor rooted in service.

Exactly one year later, the world was hit by the COVID-19 pandemic, prompting a global pause—a sacred time for humanity to confront the issues we had long considered ourselves too busy to address. During a one-week vacation that began on September 5, 2020, an unexpected turn of events led to a 16-week adventure. Virtual lockdown in Washington, D.C., could not compete with the allure of affordable room rates and an uninhabited two-mile stretch of pristine tropical beach. In April 2021, an incredible opportunity presented itself when I was granted the privilege of living and working at the very resort where I had found solace—a tranquil existence in Paradise. In this role, I elevated the team's service level and enriched the guest experience. However, my tenure unexpectedly came to an end in March 2023. Although it wasn't part of my plan, I trust that once again, God's wisdom surpasses my own. I have been divinely healed from the losses life has dealt me—the loss of Leo, my beloved partner, and the departure from a job I adored. Now, I embark on my true purpose—the work I was meant to do.

Allow me to introduce myself. My name is Tina Hamm, and I am a luxury travel concierge, podcaster, author, and international motivational speaker. Through life's trials and tribulations, I have gained invaluable wisdom, honed my ability to articulate my experiences, and discovered a gift for resonating with and inspiring others. This is the life I was born to live, and I invite you to stay tuned as I continue to unfold my purpose and share my journey with the world.

Sunny regards from Paradise
Tina Hamm.

SELF CARE IS THE NEW SEXY THE RETREAT

July 27-31, 2023

Simpson Bay Resort St. Maarten

**A wellness retreat for women
who are operating
on fumes and are ready to fill up**

LIMITED SPOTS AVAILABLE

www.selfcareisthenewsexytheretreat.com

During the acute phase of my illness I lost 50 pounds, something I had hoped to do for years, but not in such a painful and unhealthy way. I began to pay attention to every ingredient that I put in my body so that my digestive system could heal. As my nutrition and gut health improved, I could move again. I began with very slow walks with my family in our neighborhood, where I met my retired neighbor who is a run coach. She encouraged me to start running. We gradually built up my running stamina and I completed two marathons last year. Moving my body became a celebration and helps me relieve stress. It's been a journey of learning what works best for me and now my focus is maintaining good wellness. I am on a mission to encourage everyone to actively invest in self-care every day. Self-care is not selfish. I learned the hard way that I could not continue to repress emotions and avoid taking care of myself - it certainly caught up with me. You can't drive a car without fuel and you can't fully enjoy your life or maximize your impact if you don't prioritize self-care.

It took a medical crisis for me to get serious about self-care.

The Wellness Journey of Jamie Sanderson Reid

Out of nowhere, I was knocked off my feet with crippling symptoms that left me wiped out and fearful for my future. When I finally received the diagnosis of ulcerative colitis, it was a relief to have some answer to what was going on with me. I believe that stress and inflammation was building up in my lower intestines for years. Up until that point, I was always procrastinating about health and wellness. I would invest in myself for a short spurt, but then give up when responsibilities and stress piled up. After getting so sick that I could not stand up without being exhausted, I finally opened my eyes and realized that I had to prioritize taking care of myself and I could not put it off another day. By the grace of God I improved.

Power to Win at Fitness
Planner with Devotional

This book is designed as an 8-week evidenced based program because this time frame is an ideal amount of time to implement strategies for your goals and assess your progress.

Powertowinatfitness@gmail.com
@powertowinatfitness

RESOURCES

FEATURED RESOURCES

Domestic violence is a systematic way to destroy a woman from the inside out – Dr. Shana

Domestic violence is a pervasive problem that affects women in various ways, extending beyond physical abuse. Women can be subjected to emotional, financial, mental, psychological, sexual, or physical abuse. It is important to recognize that when a woman is in an abusive situation, the focus should not be on why she doesn't leave but rather why the abuser doesn't stop the abuse.

Dr. Shana, as the founder of Her VOICE, a non-profit organization committed to empowering survivors of domestic violence through mentorship and education, understands the profound impact of abuse on women. It can lead to depression, anxiety, and a loss of self, resulting in low self-esteem and confidence. Drawing upon her clinical expertise as a mental health professional, she aims to help survivors regain their well-being and return to a healthy level of functioning.

Since 2014, Her VOICE has played a crucial role in the Houston, Texas community, providing support to domestic violence survivors through a community-based mentorship program. Similar to the concept of Big Brothers, Big Sisters, this program pairs survivors together for support. Given that 1 in 5 women face severe physical violence and approximately half of women experience psychological abuse, the work of Her VOICE is both necessary and impactful.

The World Health Organization reports that around 30% of women globally suffer from domestic violence. As Dr. Shana planned to bring the "Self Care is the New Sexy Retreat" to the beautiful island of St. Maarten, she prioritized connecting with local domestic violence organizations to increase awareness and provide support. Safe Haven, one of the island's domestic violence programs, offers shelter, education, and support for survivors. Dr. Shana is deeply committed to ensuring that women worldwide have access to the necessary resources for their emotional and physical well-being when faced with a violent relationship.

It is essential to recognize that surviving a domestic violent relationship does not define a woman's identity or limit her potential. With the right support and resources, she can reclaim her life, well-being, and future.

For more information or support in Houston, TX visit www.her-voice.net

Dr. Shana D. Lewis is the founder and Board President of Her VOICE, a Texas based non profit organization that supports domestic violence survivors. She is a global domestic violence expert and advocate who is dedicating to helping women stay out of the cycle of violence.

International Resource (St. Marteen)

About the Safe Haven Foundation

The Safe Haven Foundation was founded in 1998, and is a non-profit organization located on Sint Maarten, that operates the only shelter on the Dutch side of the island, dedicated to women and their minor children, in need of a safe space to escape domestic abuse conditions, and gain access to services such as referrals and psychosocial support, via our strong working relationships and collaboration with judicial organizations, and social support services within the chain of domestic violence partners and stakeholders.

The Safe Haven Board and Staff are dedicated to providing compassionate, confidential, and sustainable services, by providing personalized care in line with individual needs, and constant opportunities for growth, in a professional and supportive environment, giving survivors encouragement and hope to heal from the trauma and injustice that they have been subjected to.

Our community-based programs, such as our Self-Esteem Workshops, Mediation sessions, Safe Homes Training sessions, Youth Empowerment programs, and Community Talks programs, also allows us to spread awareness and educate persons in the community about domestic abuse, in order to collectively diminish the levels and effects of domestic abuse on our island.

Contact information:
Hotline: 9333
Phone: +1-721-523-6400
Email: info@safehavensxm.sx
www.safehavensxm.sx
Facebook: @SafeHavenfoundationsxm

Distress Tolerance & Mindfulness Tools: A Brief Guide to Stay Present and Grounded

The book is a great resource and overview to explain and explore how people are not born with coping or mindfulness skills. Instead, we learn them over time. These skills are essential during all stages of our life. They offer many benefits including to help us get through difficult situations, to stay focused and enjoy being present in the moment, and so much more. This book will discuss practical information about mental health awareness and provide strategies and skills to improve distress tolerance and mindfulness.

Available on Amazon.com

Aid to victims of Domestic Violence

1001 Texas Ave #600, Houston, TX, 77002 - 713-224-9911

Call Mon- Fri 8am – 5pm
24 hours national Domestic violence hotline (1-800-799-safe) (7233)
· Free legal Aid services
· Battering Intervention
· Prevention Program
· Education services
· Gain access to community resources
· Gain Access to mental health services
· Addiction Treatment program
· Housing program
· Mental Health services

Avda.org
Twitter @AVDAcommits
IG @AVDA_TX

S.M.O.O.O.T.H. [Speaking Mentally, Outwardly Opening Opportunities Toward Healing

S.M.O.O.O.T.H. is a non-profit organization that leads the way to empower women affected by the perils of domestic violence. We believe that those overcoming abuses are unique and deserve a multi-pronged approach when being engaged.

We connect Survivors to reputable community resources (Counseling, Internships, Personal + Mental Health, Legal) and provide our Butterflies with emotional and financial assistance.

www.smooothinc.org/contact

Crack The Speaker Code Workbook

Understand your value and worth. Show up in the world. This resource will get you there and keep you there.

GraceLHolden@gmail.com
facebook.com/graceLholdengrace

NOTES TO Save Myself:

Reflect on what you've read. What stands out to you?

NOTES TO 

What action steps will you take from what you've read?